How will you reach your next summit?

Jo –
It's About
Momentum!

Until one is committed, there is hesitancy, the chance to draw back, always ineffectiveness concerning all acts of initiative and creation. There is one elementary truth, the ignorance of which kills countless ideas and splendid plans; that the moment one definitely commits oneself, then providence moves too. All sorts of things occur to help one that would never otherwise have occurred. A whole stream of events issues from the decision raising in one's favor all manner of unforeseen events, meetings and material assistance which no one could have dreamed would have come their way. I have learned a deep respect for one of Goethe's couplets: "Whatever you can do or dream you can, begin it. Boldness has genius, power and magic in it. Begin it now!"

W. H. Murray

REACHING YOUR NEXT SUMMIT!

MOMENTUM PLANNER AND JOURNAL

MANLEY FEINBERG

VERTICALLESSONS.com

AM I WILLING TO COMMIT?

COMMITMENT TO THE RELENTLESS PURSUIT OF EXCELLENCE ON THE EDGE

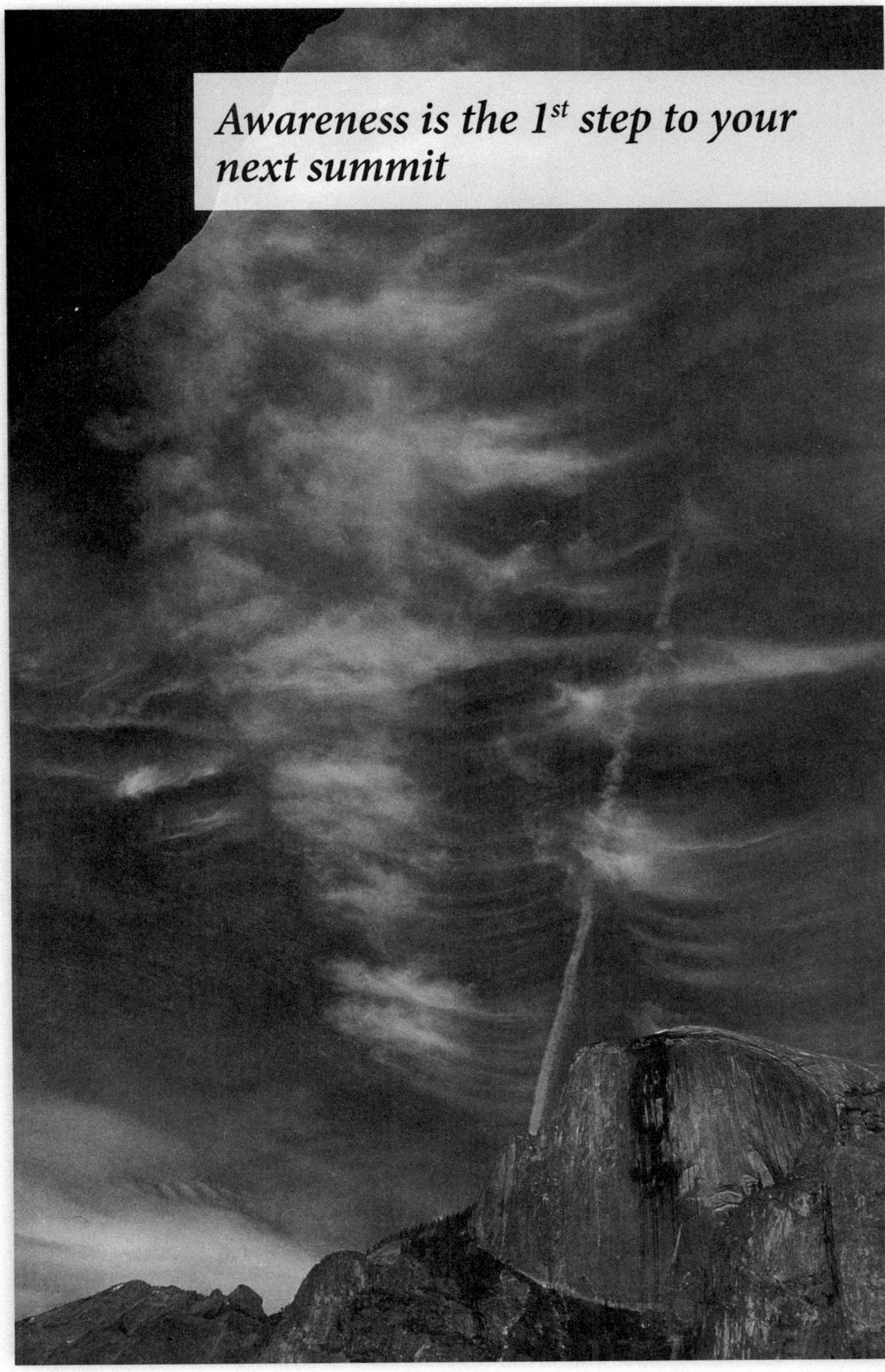
Awareness is the 1st step to your next summit

FIELD NOTES

1 DECIDE IF IT'S WORTH IT

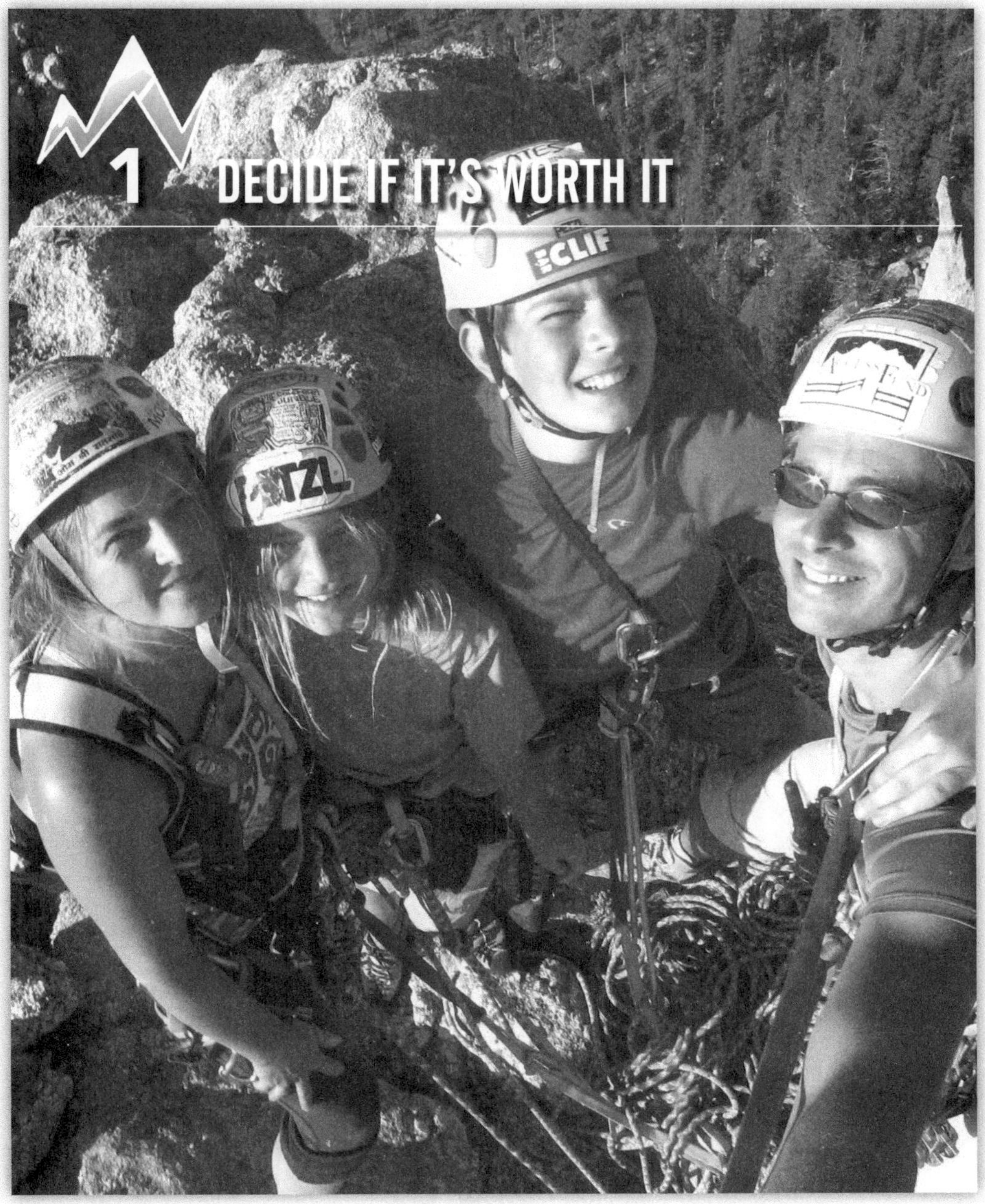

CLARIFY THE MOUNTAIN

SUMMIT

NOW

WORKSHEET – IS IT WORTH IT?

My next summit is:

When I reach the summit, I imagine the following view, feeling, and new perspective:

Reaching the next summit will serve the following people:

Imagine an encounter in the future with someone your courageous effort helps. What do they say to you when they thank you and share how you've helped them with your efforts?

From my next summit, I will probably be able to see the following possibilities and next summits:

My next summit will be worth it because:

FIELD NOTES

2 DECLARE YOUR CURRENT CLIMB

1. Declare only one initiative as your Current Climb

What are possible Current Climbs?

2. Select your Current Climb

How committed am *I?*

How committed are *we?*

What will it take for me to say with conviction, *"No matter what, I'm going to move this forward every day!"*

3. Build and Maintain Momentum

What will I do to Build *Massive Momentum*?

4. Visibility Drives Velocity

How will *I* keep *my* Current Climb Visible?

How will *we* keep *our* Current Climb Visible?

EMOTIONAL GRAVITY

What could be dragging me down? (barriers, fear)

What is amplifying Emotional Gravity for me?

What helps me feel free, light, in the zone or in flow? (safe state of mind, importance vs urgency, edge of your comfort zone, breakthrough results, why worth pursuing; it is emotionally palpable and crystal clear)

Embrace Exposure

What uncomfortable opportunity is presenting today?

What will be possible when I ________________________________?

"Action conquers fear."
Peter Nivio Zarlenga

FIELD NOTES

FIELD NOTES

3 GET ON BELAY!

Who do I need On Belay today to do what I need to do?

Who do I trust most?

Who do I need to trust more?

Who do I need OFF belay?

Who will I belay today?

Who am I going to reach out to with intention?

Get On Belay! Constantly.

Embrace Exposure

Photo by Eric Draper

FIELD NOTES

4 CELEBRATE THE SUMMITS!

Celebrate all summits, big and small everyday

Celebrating summits builds momentum

- **Celebrate big, but briefly**
- **Perspective is power**

Call back to your last summit in your next struggle

1. **Choose a significant struggle in which you eventually succeeded.**

2. **Write or verbally relive it.**

3. **Relive the emotions of fear and frustration when you were ready to give up.**

4. **Relive the summit celebration moment.**

5. **Then commit to one small and low resistance action toward your next summit.**

How will you start the climb to your next summit?

What is at least one Vertical Lesson you will commit to work on starting now?

MY 7 SUMMIT AFFIRMATIONS

What good is a wind without a compass?

Seneca

FIELD NOTES

5 MASTER THE ART OF THE RESTART

VERTICAL MOMENTUM – MASTER THE ART OF THE *MAJOR RESTART*

Recover – be intentional

- **Beware and be ready to examine why it's worth it for you to take time to recover**

Reset – Stop before you start.

- **Is this still serving me?**
- **If no, what could it make room for?**
- **What in my life is most draining?**

If you can't commit to stopping, give yourself permission to procrastinate a restart of the activity.

Procrastination can be a powerful tool when used intentionally.

Re-energize – Embrace renewal activities guilt-free

- **What can you indulge in, even if for just a few hours, for a few days in a row that re-energizes you?**
- **Whom can you connect with in life who gives you energy and makes you feel whole again?**
- **What book, movie, or event, could you attend that helps you fil up your energy tank with inspiration?**

Regain Momentum – Master the Art of the Restart *Day-to-Day*

Essential Vertical Mindset: *Expect to fall*

1. **Recall a previous summit:** Call back to your last summit in your next struggle

2. **Re-examine:** Figure out your next move

3. **Restart:** Get on with it before you are ready 100% ready

Outrageous optimism
Perspective fuels optimism

What do you need to restart?

What would help you re-commit?

You only need to know a couple of moves – not a whole plan – restart before ready!

Photo by Eric Draper

List a few of your undone projects, goals, ideas, etc. In the space provided, write a list that references things you have started but not finished or things you want to start and just haven't gotten started...

Project(s)/ Climb/Goals/ Commit/Focus	Recover	Reset	Re-Energize	Regain Momentum

Photo by Mr. Way

FIELD NOTES

REFLECTION > CLARITY > MOMENTUM

Consistently, ask yourself these Essential Questions and write your responses in the space provided. *When you go Deeper, You Climb Higher.*

What am I Grateful for?

What do I want More of?

Where is Resistance showing up in my life?

What might I be holding onto that I need to let go of?

What do I need to Restart?

What uncomfortable opportunity is presenting today?

Who am I Grateful for?

MY 7 SUMMIT AFFIRMATIONS

The trouble is, you think you have time.

Buddha

FIELD NOTES

Perspective Fuels Optimism

MONTH:

MONDAY	TUESDAY	WEDNESDAY	THURSDAY

FRIDAY	SATURDAY	SUNDAY	CURRENT CLIMBS

MONTH:

MONDAY	TUESDAY	WEDNESDAY	THURSDAY

FRIDAY	SATURDAY	SUNDAY	CURRENT CLIMBS

MONTH:

MONDAY	TUESDAY	WEDNESDAY	THURSDAY

FRIDAY	SATURDAY	SUNDAY	CURRENT CLIMBS

REFLECTION > CLARITY > MOMENTUM

Consistently, ask yourself these Essential Questions and write your responses in the space provided. *When you go Deeper, You Climb Higher.*

What am I Grateful for?

What do I want More of?

Where is Resistance showing up in my life?

What might I be holding onto that I need to let go of?

What do I need to Restart?

What uncomfortable opportunity is presenting today?

Who am I Grateful for?

MY 7 SUMMIT AFFIRMATIONS

Discipline is remembering what you want.

David Campbell

Today I am grateful for . . . Date:

1

2

3

Today I am feeling . . .

Declare My Current Climb:

My 3 Summit Focus

3 MIT: (Most Important Task)

1

2

3

Get On Belay

Who do *I* need *On Belay* today?

Who needs *Me On Belay* today?

Act as if what you do makes a difference. It does.

William James

Tonight I am grateful for . . .

1

2

3

Tonight I am gaining clarity on . . .

6 Clarity

7

8

9

10

11

12 Momentum

1

2

3

4

5

6

7

8

9 Reflection

Uncomfortable, But Worth it:

Celebrate the Summits:

Lessons Learned / *Next Time:*

Today I am grateful for . . . **Date:**..........

1 ....

2 ....

3 ....

Today I am feeling . . .

....

Declare My Current Climb:..........

My 3 Summit Focus

3 MIT: (Most Important Task)

1 ....

2 ....

3 ....

Get On Belay

Who do *I* need *On Belay* today? ....

Who needs *Me On Belay* today?..........

Asking the right question about the future is more powerful than having the right answer about the past.

Mike Figliuolo

Tonight I am grateful for . . .

1 ....

2 ....

3 ....

Tonight I am gaining clarity on . . .

....

6 ....Clarity

7 ....

8 ....

9 ....

10 ....

11 ....

12 ....Momentum

1 ....

2 ....

3 ....

4 ....

5 ....

6 ....

7 ....

8 ....

9 ....Reflection

Uncomfortable, But Worth it:

Celebrate the Summits:

Lessons Learned / *Next Time:*

Today I am grateful for . . . Date: ....

1 ....

2 ....

3 ....

Today I am feeling . . .

....

Declare My Current Climb: ....

My 3 Summit Focus

3 MIT: (Most Important Task)

1 ....

2 ....

3 ....

Get On Belay

Who do *I* need *On Belay* today? ....

Who needs *Me On Belay* today? ....

Avoiding danger is no safer in the long run than outright exposure. Life is either a daring adventure, or nothing.

Helen Keller

Tonight I am grateful for . . .

1 ....

2 ....

3 ....

Tonight I am gaining clarity on . . .

....

6 Clarity

7

8

9

10

11

12 Momentum

1

2

3

4

5

6

7

8

9 Reflection

Uncomfortable, But Worth it:

Celebrate the Summits:

Lessons Learned / *Next Time:*

Today I am grateful for . . . Date:

1

2

3

Today I am feeling . . .

Declare My Current Climb:

My 3 Summit Focus

3 MIT: (Most Important Task)

1

2

3

Get On Belay

Who do *I* need *On Belay* today?

Who needs *Me On Belay* today?

Better to light one small candle than to curse the darkness.

Chinese Proverb

Tonight I am grateful for . . .

1

2

3

Tonight I am gaining clarity on . . .

6 Clarity

7

8

9

10

11

12 Momentum

1

2

3

4

5

6

7

8

9 Reflection

Uncomfortable, But Worth it:

Celebrate the Summits:

Lessons Learned / *Next Time:*

Today I am grateful for . . .   Date: ....

1 ....

2 ....

3 ....

Today I am feeling . . .

....

Declare My Current Climb: ....

My 3 Summit Focus

3 MIT: (Most Important Task)

1 ....

2 ....

3 ....

Get On Belay

Who do *I* need *On Belay* today? ....

Who needs *Me On Belay* today? ....

Beyond being rich and famous, when I got started, more than anything I wanted to be great!

Bruce Springsteen

Tonight I am grateful for . . .

1 ....

2 ....

3 ....

Tonight I am gaining clarity on . . .

....

6 Clarity

7

8

9

10

11

12 Momentum

1

2

3

4

5

6

7

8

9 Reflection

Uncomfortable, But Worth it:

Celebrate the Summits:

Lessons Learned / *Next Time:*

Today I am grateful for . . . **Date:** ....

1 ....

2 ....

3 ....

Today I am feeling . . .

....

Declare My Current Climb: ....

My 3 Summit Focus

3 MIT: (Most Important Task)

1 ....

2 ....

3 ....

Get On Belay

Who do *I* need *On Belay* today? ....

Who needs *Me On Belay* today? ....

Discipline is the bridge between goals and accomplishment.

Jim Rohn

Tonight I am grateful for . . .

1 ....

2 ....

3 ....

Tonight I am gaining clarity on . . .

....

6 Clarity

7

8

9

10

11

12 Momentum

1

2

3

4

5

6

7

8

9 Reflection

Uncomfortable, But Worth it:

Celebrate the Summits:

Lessons Learned / *Next Time:*

Today I am grateful for . . . Date: ....

1 ....

2 ....

3 ....

Today I am feeling . . .

....

Declare My Current Climb: ....

My 3 Summit Focus

3 MIT: (Most Important Task)

1 ....

2 ....

3 ....

Get On Belay

Who do *I* need *On Belay* today? ....

Who needs *Me On Belay* today? ....

Do not wait: the time will never be "just right". Start where you stand, and work whatever tools you may have at your command and better tools will be found as you go along.

Napoleon Hill

Tonight I am grateful for . . .

1 ....

2 ....

3 ....

Tonight I am gaining clarity on . . .

....

6 .... **Clarity**

7

8

9

10

11

12 .... **Momentum**

1

2

3

4

5

6

7

8

9 .... **Reflection**

Uncomfortable, But Worth it:

Celebrate the Summits:

Lessons Learned / *Next Time:*

REFLECTION > CLARITY > MOMENTUM

Consistently, ask yourself these Essential Questions and write your responses in the space provided. *When you go Deeper, You Climb Higher.*

What am I Grateful for?

What do I want More of?

Where is Resistance showing up in my life?

What might I be holding onto that I need to let go of?

What do I need to Restart?

What uncomfortable opportunity is presenting today?

Who am I Grateful for?

MY 7 SUMMIT AFFIRMATIONS

Action rides the wave of fear.

Manley Feinberg II

Today I am grateful for . . . Date: ....

1 ....

2 ....

3 ....

Today I am feeling . . .

....

Declare My Current Climb: ....

My 3 Summit Focus

3 MIT: (Most Important Task)

1 ....

2 ....

3 ....

Get On Belay

Who do *I* need *On Belay* today? ....

Who needs *Me On Belay* today? ....

Do or do not, there is no try.

Yoda

Tonight I am grateful for . . .

1 ....

2 ....

3 ....

Tonight I am gaining clarity on . . .

....

6 .... Clarity

7

8

9

10

11

12 .... Momentum

1

2

3

4

5

6

7

8

9 .... Reflection

Uncomfortable, But Worth it:

Celebrate the Summits:

Lessons Learned / *Next Time:*

Today I am grateful for . . . Date:..

1 ....

2 ....

3 ....

Today I am feeling . . .

....

Declare My Current Climb:..

My 3 Summit Focus

3 MIT: (Most Important Task)

1 ....

2 ....

3 ....

Get On Belay

Who do *I* need *On Belay* today? ....

Who needs *Me On Belay* today? ....

Dream as if you will live forever,
live as if you will die today.

James Dean

Tonight I am grateful for . . .

1 ....

2 ....

3 ....

Tonight I am gaining clarity on . . .

....

6 Clarity

7

8

9

10

11

12 Momentum

1

2

3

4

5

6

7

8

9 Reflection

Uncomfortable, But Worth it:

Celebrate the Summits:

Lessons Learned / *Next Time:*

Today I am grateful for . . . Date: ....

1 ....

2 ....

3 ....

Today I am feeling . . .

....

Declare My Current Climb: ....

My 3 Summit Focus

3 MIT: (Most Important Task)

1 ....

2 ....

3 ....

Get On Belay

Who do *I* need *On Belay* today? ....

Who needs *Me On Belay* today? ....

Even if you're on the right track, you'll get run over if you just sit there.

Will Rogers

Tonight I am grateful for . . .

1 ....

2 ....

3 ....

Tonight I am gaining clarity on . . .

....

6 Clarity

7

8

9

10

11

12 Momentum

1

2

3

4

5

6

7

8

9 Reflection

Uncomfortable, But Worth it:

Celebrate the Summits:

Lessons Learned / *Next Time:*

Today I am grateful for . . . **Date:** ....

1 ....

2 ....

3 ....

Today I am feeling . . .

....

Declare My Current Climb: ....

My 3 Summit Focus

3 MIT: (Most Important Task)

1 ....

2 ....

3 ....

Get On Belay

Who do *I* need *On Belay* today? ....

Who needs *Me On Belay* today? ....

Every time you are tempted to react in the same old way, ask if you want to be a prisoner of the past or a pioneer of the future.

Deepak Chopra

Tonight I am grateful for . . .

1 ....

2 ....

3 ....

Tonight I am gaining clarity on . . .

....

6 Clarity

7

8

9

10

11

12 Momentum

1

2

3

4

5

6

7

8

9 Reflection

Uncomfortable, But Worth it:

Celebrate the Summits:

Lessons Learned / *Next Time:*

Today I am grateful for . . . Date: ....

1 ....

2 ....

3 ....

Today I am feeling . . .

....

Declare My Current Climb: ....

My 3 Summit Focus

3 MIT: (Most Important Task)

1 ....

2 ....

3 ....

Get On Belay

Who do *I* need *On Belay* today? ....

Who needs *Me On Belay* today? ....

The more clarity you have, the more powerful your goals are.

Robert G. Allen

Tonight I am grateful for . . .

1 ....

2 ....

3 ....

Tonight I am gaining clarity on . . .

....

6 ....Clarity

7

8

9

10

11

12 ....Momentum

1

2

3

4

5

6

7

8

9 ....Reflection

Uncomfortable, But Worth it:

Celebrate the Summits:

Lessons Learned / *Next Time:*

Today I am grateful for . . . Date: ....

1 ....

2 ....

3 ....

Today I am feeling . . .

....

Declare My Current Climb: ....

My 3 Summit Focus

3 MIT: (Most Important Task)

1 ....

2 ....

3 ....

Get On Belay

Who do *I* need *On Belay* today? ....

Who needs *Me On Belay* today? ....

Everybody needs beauty as well as bread, places to play in and pray in, where nature may heal and give strength to body and soul alike. I must return to the mountains—to Yosemite.

John Muir

Tonight I am grateful for . . .

1 ....

2 ....

3 ....

Tonight I am gaining clarity on . . .

....

6 Clarity

7

8

9

10

11

12 Momentum

1

2

3

4

5

6

7

8

9 Reflection

Uncomfortable, But Worth it:

Celebrate the Summits:

Lessons Learned / *Next Time:*

Today I am grateful for . . . Date: ....

1 ....

2 ....

3 ....

Today I am feeling . . .

....

Declare My Current Climb: ....

My 3 Summit Focus

3 MIT: (Most Important Task)

1 ....

2 ....

3 ....

Get On Belay

Who do *I* need *On Belay* today? ....

Who needs *Me On Belay* today? ....

Great minds discuss ideas; average minds discuss events; small minds discuss people.

Eleanor Roosevelt

Tonight I am grateful for . . .

1 ....

2 ....

3 ....

Tonight I am gaining clarity on . . .

....

6 Clarity

7

8

9

10

11

12 Momentum

1

2

3

4

5

6

7

8

9 Reflection

Uncomfortable, But Worth it:

Celebrate the Summits:

Lessons Learned / *Next Time:*

REFLECTION > CLARITY > MOMENTUM

Consistently, ask yourself these Essential Questions and write your responses in the space provided. *When you go Deeper, You Climb Higher.*

What am I Grateful for?

What do I want More of?

Where is Resistance showing up in my life?

What might I be holding onto that I need to let go of?

What do I need to Restart?

What uncomfortable opportunity is presenting today?

Who am I Grateful for?

MY 7 SUMMIT AFFIRMATIONS

Belief is the basis for all things possible.

Manley Feinberg II

Today I am grateful for . . . Date: ....

1 ....

2 ....

3 ....

Today I am feeling . . .

....

Declare My Current Climb: ....

My 3 Summit Focus

3 MIT: (Most Important Task)

1 ....

2 ....

3 ....

Get On Belay

Who do *I* need *On Belay* today? ....

Who needs *Me On Belay* today? ....

Habits are like train tracks. They take a long time to put in place, but once you do, they will take you anywhere you want to go.

Patricia Fripp

Tonight I am grateful for . . .

1 ....

2 ....

3 ....

Tonight I am gaining clarity on . . .

....

6 Clarity
7
8
9
10
11
12 Momentum
1
2
3
4
5
6
7
8
9 Reflection

Uncomfortable, But Worth it:

Celebrate the Summits:

Lessons Learned / *Next Time:*

Today I am grateful for . . . Date: ....

1 ....

2 ....

3 ....

Today I am feeling . . .

....

Declare My Current Climb: ....

My 3 Summit Focus

3 MIT: (Most Important Task)

1 ....

2 ....

3 ....

Get On Belay

Who do *I* need *On Belay* today? ....

Who needs *Me On Belay* today? ....

Have a day that changes tomorrow.

Michael W. Glover

Tonight I am grateful for . . .

1 ....

2 ....

3 ....

Tonight I am gaining clarity on . . .

....

6 Clarity

7

8

9

10

11

12 Momentum

1

2

3

4

5

6

7

8

9 Reflection

Uncomfortable, But Worth it:

Celebrate the Summits:

Lessons Learned / *Next Time:*

Today I am grateful for . . . **Date:**..........

1 ....

2 ....

3 ....

Today I am feeling . . .

....

Declare My Current Climb:..........

My 3 Summit Focus

3 MIT: (Most Important Task)

1 ....

2 ....

3 ....

Get On Belay

Who do *I* need *On Belay* today? ....

Who needs *Me On Belay* today?..........

Here's how I am going to beat you. I'm going to out work you. That's it. That's all there is to it.

Pat Summitt

Tonight I am grateful for . . .

1 ....

2 ....

3 ....

Tonight I am gaining clarity on . . .

....

6 Clarity

7

8

9

10

11

12 Momentum

1

2

3

4

5

6

7

8

9 Reflection

Uncomfortable, But Worth it:

Celebrate the Summits:

Lessons Learned / *Next Time:*

Today I am grateful for . . . Date: ....

1 ....

2 ....

3 ....

Today I am feeling . . .

....

Declare My Current Climb: ....

My 3 Summit Focus

3 MIT: (Most Important Task)

1 ....

2 ....

3 ....

Get On Belay

Who do *I* need *On Belay* today? ....

Who needs *Me On Belay* today? ....

Hope in the future gives you power in the present.

Les Brown

Tonight I am grateful for . . .

1 ....

2 ....

3 ....

Tonight I am gaining clarity on . . .

....

6 Clarity

7

8

9

10

11

12 Momentum

1

2

3

4

5

6

7

8

9 Reflection

Uncomfortable, But Worth it:

Celebrate the Summits:

Lessons Learned / *Next Time:*

Today I am grateful for . . . **Date:** ....

1 ....

2 ....

3 ....

Today I am feeling . . .

....

Declare My Current Climb: ....

My 3 Summit Focus

3 MIT: (Most Important Task)

1 ....

2 ....

3 ....

Get On Belay

Who do *I* need *On Belay* today? ....

Who needs *Me On Belay* today? ....

I hated every minute of training, but I said, "Don't quit. Suffer now and live the rest of your life as a champion."

Muhammad Ali

Tonight I am grateful for . . .

1 ....

2 ....

3 ....

Tonight I am gaining clarity on . . .

....

6 .... **Clarity**

7

8

9

10

11

12 .... **Momentum**

1

2

3

4

5

6

7

8

9 .... **Reflection**

Uncomfortable, But Worth it:

Celebrate the Summits:

Lessons Learned / *Next Time:*

Today I am grateful for . . . **Date:**..................................

1 ....

2 ....

3 ....

Today I am feeling . . .

....

Declare My Current Climb:..................................

My 3 Summit Focus

3 MIT: (Most Important Task)

1 ....

2 ....

3 ....

Get On Belay

Who do *I* need *On Belay* today? ....

Who needs *Me On Belay* today?..................................

I have been impressed with the urgency of doing. Knowing is not enough; we must apply. Being willing is not enough; we must do.

Leonardo Da Vinci

Tonight I am grateful for . . .

1 ....

2 ....

3 ....

Tonight I am gaining clarity on . . .

....

6 .... **Clarity**

7

8

9

10

11

12 .... **Momentum**

1

2

3

4

5

6

7

8

9 .... **Reflection**

Uncomfortable, But Worth it:

Celebrate the Summits:

Lessons Learned / *Next Time:*

Today I am grateful for . . . Date: ....

1 ....

2 ....

3 ....

Today I am feeling . . .

....

Declare My Current Climb: ....

My 3 Summit Focus

3 MIT: (Most Important Task)

1 ....

2 ....

3 ....

Get On Belay

Who do *I* need *On Belay* today? ....

Who needs *Me On Belay* today? ....

I work as hard as I have to in order to achieve my vision of what I know is possible.

Jamey Andreas

Tonight I am grateful for . . .

1 ....

2 ....

3 ....

Tonight I am gaining clarity on . . .

....

6 .... Clarity

7

8

9

10

11

12 .... Momentum

1

2

3

4

5

6

7

8

9 .... Reflection

Uncomfortable, But Worth it:

Celebrate the Summits:

Lessons Learned / *Next Time:*

REFLECTION > CLARITY > MOMENTUM

Consistently, ask yourself these Essential Questions and write your responses in the space provided. *When you go Deeper, You Climb Higher.*

What am I Grateful for?

What do I want More of?

Where is Resistance showing up in my life?

What might I be holding onto that I need to let go of?

What do I need to Restart?

What uncomfortable opportunity is presenting today?

Who am I Grateful for?

MY 7 SUMMIT AFFIRMATIONS

Beliefs build prisons and palaces, boundaries and breakthroughs.

Manley Feinberg II

Today I am grateful for . . . Date:

1

2

3

Today I am feeling . . .

Declare My Current Climb:

My 3 Summit Focus

3 MIT: (Most Important Task)

1

2

3

Get On Belay

Who do *I* need *On Belay* today?

Who needs *Me On Belay* today?

Don't get ready, stay ready.

Craig Valentine

Tonight I am grateful for . . .

1

2

3

Tonight I am gaining clarity on . . .

6 Clarity

7

8

9

10

11

12 Momentum

1

2

3

4

5

6

7

8

9 Reflection

Uncomfortable, But Worth it:

Celebrate the Summits:

Lessons Learned / *Next Time:*

Today I am grateful for . . . Date: ....

1 ....

2 ....

3 ....

Today I am feeling . . .

....

Declare My Current Climb: ....

My 3 Summit Focus

3 MIT: (Most Important Task)

1 ....

2 ....

3 ....

Get On Belay

Who do *I* need *On Belay* today? ....

Who needs *Me On Belay* today? ....

Ideas are free, execution is priceless.

Scott Ginsburg

Tonight I am grateful for . . .

1 ....

2 ....

3 ....

Tonight I am gaining clarity on . . .

....

6 .... **Clarity**

7

8

9

10

11

12 .... **Momentum**

1

2

3

4

5

6

7

8

9 .... **Reflection**

Uncomfortable, But Worth it:

Celebrate the Summits:

Lessons Learned / *Next Time:*

Today I am grateful for . . . Date: ....

1 ....
2 ....
3 ....

Today I am feeling . . .

....

Declare My Current Climb: ....

My 3 Summit Focus

3 MIT: (Most Important Task)

1 ....
2 ....
3 ....

Get On Belay

Who do *I* need *On Belay* today? ....

Who needs *Me On Belay* today? ....

If I had eight hours to chop down a tree, I'd spend six sharpening my axe.

Abraham Lincoln

Tonight I am grateful for . . .

1 ....
2 ....
3 ....

Tonight I am gaining clarity on . . .

....

6 Clarity

7

8

9

10

11

12 Momentum

1

2

3

4

5

6

7

8

9 Reflection

Uncomfortable, But Worth it:

Celebrate the Summits:

Lessons Learned / *Next Time:*

Today I am grateful for . . . Date:

1 ....

2 ....

3 ....

Today I am feeling . . .

....

Declare My Current Climb: ....

My 3 Summit Focus

3 MIT: (Most Important Task)

1 ....

2 ....

3 ....

Get On Belay

Who do *I* need *On Belay* today? ....

Who needs *Me On Belay* today? ....

If you are patient in one moment of anger, you will avoid one hundred days of sorrow.

Chinese Proverb

Tonight I am grateful for . . .

1 ....

2 ....

3 ....

Tonight I am gaining clarity on . . .

....

6 .... Clarity

7

8

9

10

11

12 .... Momentum

1

2

3

4

5

6

7

8

9 .... Reflection

Uncomfortable, But Worth it:

Celebrate the Summits:

Lessons Learned / *Next Time:*

Today I am grateful for . . .   Date: ....

1 ....

2 ....

3 ....

Today I am feeling . . .

....

Declare My Current Climb: ....

My 3 Summit Focus

3 MIT: (Most Important Task)

1 ....

2 ....

3 ....

Get On Belay

Who do *I* need *On Belay* today? ....

Who needs *Me On Belay* today? ....

If you do a little at a time, you always get done.

Jeff Dickerson's neighbor, a minister of wisdom

Tonight I am grateful for . . .

1 ....

2 ....

3 ....

Tonight I am gaining clarity on . . .

....

6 Clarity

7

8

9

10

11

12 Momentum

1

2

3

4

5

6

7

8

9 Reflection

Uncomfortable, But Worth it:

Celebrate the Summits:

Lessons Learned / *Next Time:*

Today I am grateful for . . . Date: ....

1 ....

2 ....

3 ....

Today I am feeling . . .

....

Declare My Current Climb: ....

My 3 Summit Focus

3 MIT: (Most Important Task)

1 ....

2 ....

3 ....

Get On Belay

Who do *I* need *On Belay* today? ....

Who needs *Me On Belay* today? ....

If you learn how to control your mind,
anything is possible.

Wim Hof

Tonight I am grateful for . . .

1 ....

2 ....

3 ....

Tonight I am gaining clarity on . . .

....

6 .... Clarity

7

8

9

10

11

12 .... Momentum

1

2

3

4

5

6

7

8

9 .... Reflection

Uncomfortable, But Worth it:

Celebrate the Summits:

Lessons Learned / *Next Time:*

Today I am grateful for . . . Date:..........

1 ....

2 ....

3 ....

Today I am feeling . . .

....

Declare My Current Climb:..........

My 3 Summit Focus

3 MIT: (Most Important Task)

1 ....

2 ....

3 ....

Get On Belay

Who do *I* need *On Belay* today? ....

Who needs *Me On Belay* today?..........

If you want small changes, work on your behavior; if you want quantum-leap changes, work on your paradigms.

Stephen Covey

Tonight I am grateful for . . .

1 ....

2 ....

3 ....

Tonight I am gaining clarity on . . .

....

6 Clarity

7

8

9

10

11

12 Momentum

1

2

3

4

5

6

7

8

9 Reflection

Uncomfortable, But Worth it:

Celebrate the Summits:

Lessons Learned / *Next Time:*

REFLECTION > CLARITY > MOMENTUM

Consistently, ask yourself these Essential Questions and write your responses in the space provided. *When you go Deeper, You Climb Higher.*

What am I Grateful for?

What do I want More of?

Where is Resistance showing up in my life?

What might I be holding onto that I need to let go of?

What do I need to Restart?

What uncomfortable opportunity is presenting today?

Who am I Grateful for?

MY 7 SUMMIT AFFIRMATIONS

Clarity paves the path of consistency.

Manley Feinberg II

Today I am grateful for . . . **Date:**

1

2

3

Today I am feeling . . .

Declare My Current Climb:

My 3 Summit Focus

3 MIT: (Most Important Task)

1

2

3

Get On Belay

Who do *I* need *On Belay* today?

Who needs *Me On Belay* today?

If you're not saying "HELL YEAH!" about something, say "NO."

Derek Sivers

Tonight I am grateful for . . .

1

2

3

Tonight I am gaining clarity on . . .

6 Clarity

7

8

9

10

11

12 Momentum

1

2

3

4

5

6

7

8

9 Reflection

Uncomfortable, But Worth it:

Celebrate the Summits:

Lessons Learned / *Next Time:*

Today I am grateful for . . . Date: ....

1 ....

2 ....

3 ....

Today I am feeling . . .

....

Declare My Current Climb: ....

My 3 Summit Focus

3 MIT: (Most Important Task)

1 ....

2 ....

3 ....

Get On Belay

Who do *I* need *On Belay* today? ....

Who needs *Me On Belay* today? ....

In business, what doesn't get done today can be done tommorow. But with family, what doesn't get done today is gone forever!

Rory Vadon

Tonight I am grateful for . . .

1 ....

2 ....

3 ....

Tonight I am gaining clarity on . . .

....

6 Clarity

7

8

9

10

11

12 Momentum

1

2

3

4

5

6

7

8

9 Reflection

Uncomfortable, But Worth it:

Celebrate the Summits:

Lessons Learned / *Next Time:*

Today I am grateful for . . . Date: ....

1 ....

2 ....

3 ....

Today I am feeling . . .

....

Declare My Current Climb: ....

My 3 Summit Focus

3 MIT: (Most Important Task)

1 ....

2 ....

3 ....

Get On Belay

Who do *I* need *On Belay* today? ....

Who needs *Me On Belay* today? ....

In the midst of chaos, there is also opportunity.

Sun Tzu

Tonight I am grateful for . . .

1 ....

2 ....

3 ....

Tonight I am gaining clarity on . . .

....

6 Clarity

7

8

9

10

11

12 Momentum

1

2

3

4

5

6

7

8

9 Reflection

Uncomfortable, But Worth it:

Celebrate the Summits:

Lessons Learned / *Next Time:*

Today I am grateful for . . . **Date:** ....

1 ....

2 ....

3 ....

Today I am feeling . . .

....

Declare My Current Climb: ....

My 3 Summit Focus

3 MIT: (Most Important Task)

1 ....

2 ....

3 ....

Get On Belay

Who do *I* need *On Belay* today? ....

Who needs *Me On Belay* today? ....

It has been my observation that most people get ahead during the time that others waste.

Henry Ford

Tonight I am grateful for . . .

1 ....

2 ....

3 ....

Tonight I am gaining clarity on . . .

....

6 Clarity

7

8

9

10

11

12 Momentum

1

2

3

4

5

6

7

8

9 Reflection

Uncomfortable, But Worth it:

Celebrate the Summits:

Lessons Learned / *Next Time:*

Today I am grateful for . . . Date:........................

1 ....

2 ....

3 ....

Today I am feeling . . .

....

Declare My Current Climb:........................

My 3 Summit Focus

3 MIT: (Most Important Task)

1 ....

2 ....

3 ....

Get On Belay

Who do *I* need *On Belay* today? ....

Who needs *Me On Belay* today?........................

It's in your moments of decision that your destiny is shaped. Choose wisely.

Tony Robbins

Tonight I am grateful for . . .

1 ....

2 ....

3 ....

Tonight I am gaining clarity on . . .

....

6 .... **Clarity**

7

8

9

10

11

12 .... **Momentum**

1

2

3

4

5

6

7

8

9 .... **Reflection**

Uncomfortable, But Worth it:

Celebrate the Summits:

Lessons Learned / *Next Time:*

Today I am grateful for . . . Date:

1 ....

2 ....

3 ....

Today I am feeling . . .

....

Declare My Current Climb:..........

My 3 Summit Focus

3 MIT: (Most Important Task)

1 ....

2 ....

3 ....

Get On Belay

Who do *I* need *On Belay* today? ....

Who needs *Me On Belay* today?..........

Keep away from people who try to belittle your ambition. Small people always do that, but the really great make you feel that you too can become great.

Mark Twain

Tonight I am grateful for . . .

1 ....

2 ....

3 ....

Tonight I am gaining clarity on . . .

....

6 Clarity

7

8

9

10

11

12 Momentum

1

2

3

4

5

6

7

8

9 Reflection

Uncomfortable, But Worth it:

Celebrate the Summits:

Lessons Learned / *Next Time:*

Today I am grateful for . . . **Date:** ....

1 ....

2 ....

3 ....

Today I am feeling . . .

....

Declare My Current Climb: ....

My 3 Summit Focus

3 MIT: (Most Important Task)

1 ....

2 ....

3 ....

Get On Belay

Who do *I* need *On Belay* today? ....

Who needs *Me On Belay* today? ....

Let no one ever come to you without leaving better and happier. Be the living expression of God's kindness: kindness in your face, kindness in your eyes, kindness in your smile.

Mother Teresa

Tonight I am grateful for . . .

1 ....

2 ....

3 ....

Tonight I am gaining clarity on . . .

....

6 .... Clarity

7 ....

8 ....

9 ....

10 ....

11 ....

12 .... Momentum

1 ....

2 ....

3 ....

4 ....

5 ....

6 ....

7 ....

8 ....

9 .... Reflection

Uncomfortable, But Worth it:

Celebrate the Summits:

Lessons Learned / *Next Time:*

REFLECTION > CLARITY > MOMENTUM

Consistently, ask yourself these Essential Questions and write your responses in the space provided. *When you go Deeper, You Climb Higher.*

What am I Grateful for?

What do I want More of?

Where is Resistance showing up in my life?

What might I be holding onto that I need to let go of?

What do I need to Restart?

What uncomfortable opportunity is presenting today?

Who am I Grateful for?

MY 7 SUMMIT AFFIRMATIONS

Fear, uncertainty and discomfort are your compasses toward growth.

Manley Feinberg II

Today I am grateful for . . . **Date:**

1

2

3

Today I am feeling . . .

Declare My Current Climb:

My 3 Summit Focus

3 MIT: (Most Important Task)

1

2

3

Get On Belay

Who do *I* need *On Belay* today?

Who needs *Me On Belay* today?

Life is really simple, but we insist on making it complicated.

Confucius

Tonight I am grateful for . . .

1

2

3

Tonight I am gaining clarity on . . .

6 Clarity

7

8

9

10

11

12 Momentum

1

2

3

4

5

6

7

8

9 Reflection

Uncomfortable, But Worth it:

Celebrate the Summits:

Lessons Learned / *Next Time:*

Today I am grateful for . . . Date: ....

1 ....

2 ....

3 ....

Today I am feeling . . .

....

Declare My Current Climb: ....

My 3 Summit Focus

3 MIT: (Most Important Task)

1 ....

2 ....

3 ....

Get On Belay

Who do *I* need *On Belay* today? ....

Who needs *Me On Belay* today? ....

Never mistake MOTION for ACTION.

Ernest Hemingway

Tonight I am grateful for . . .

1 ....

2 ....

3 ....

Tonight I am gaining clarity on . . .

....

6 Clarity
7
8
9
10
11
12 Momentum
1
2
3
4
5
6
7
8
9 Reflection

Uncomfortable, But Worth it:

Celebrate the Summits:

Lessons Learned / *Next Time:*

Today I am grateful for . . . Date: ....

1 ....

2 ....

3 ....

Today I am feeling . . .

....

Declare My Current Climb: ....

My 3 Summit Focus

3 MIT: (Most Important Task)

1 ....

2 ....

3 ....

Get On Belay

Who do *I* need *On Belay* today? ....

Who needs *Me On Belay* today? ....

No one ever achieved greatness by playing it safe.

Harry Gray

Tonight I am grateful for . . .

1 ....

2 ....

3 ....

Tonight I am gaining clarity on . . .

....

6 Clarity

7

8

9

10

11

12 Momentum

1

2

3

4

5

6

7

8

9 Reflection

Uncomfortable, But Worth it:

Celebrate the Summits:

Lessons Learned / *Next Time:*

Today I am grateful for . . . **Date:** ....

1 ....

2 ....

3 ....

Today I am feeling . . .

....

Declare My Current Climb: ....

My 3 Summit Focus

3 MIT: (Most Important Task)

1 ....

2 ....

3 ....

Get On Belay

Who do *I* need *On Belay* today? ....

Who needs *Me On Belay* today? ....

No one will steal my joy. If you want to attack what we're doing, be nasty about it, have at it. You're not stealing my joy.

Coach John Calipari

Tonight I am grateful for . . .

1 ....

2 ....

3 ....

Tonight I am gaining clarity on . . .

....

6 Clarity

7

8

9

10

11

12 Momentum

1

2

3

4

5

6

7

8

9 Reflection

Uncomfortable, But Worth it:

Celebrate the Summits:

Lessons Learned / *Next Time:*

Today I am grateful for . . . Date: ....

1 ....

2 ....

3 ....

Today I am feeling . . .

....

Declare My Current Climb: ....

My 3 Summit Focus

3 MIT: (Most Important Task)

1 ....

2 ....

3 ....

Get On Belay

Who do *I* need *On Belay* today? ....

Who needs *Me On Belay* today? ....

When you are consistent, committed and steady your goals become your reality.

Sam Silverstein

Tonight I am grateful for . . .

1 ....

2 ....

3 ....

Tonight I am gaining clarity on . . .

....

6 .... **Clarity**

7

8

9

10

11

12 .... **Momentum**

1

2

3

4

5

6

7

8

9 .... **Reflection**

Uncomfortable, But Worth it:

Celebrate the Summits:

Lessons Learned / *Next Time:*

Today I am grateful for . . . Date: ....

1 ....

2 ....

3 ....

Today I am feeling . . .

....

Declare My Current Climb: ....

My 3 Summit Focus

3 MIT: (Most Important Task)

1 ....

2 ....

3 ....

Get On Belay

Who do *I* need *On Belay* today? ....

Who needs *Me On Belay* today? ....

One more question can be the turning point.

Maxine Clark

Tonight I am grateful for . . .

1 ....

2 ....

3 ....

Tonight I am gaining clarity on . . .

....

6 Clarity

7

8

9

10

11

12 Momentum

1

2

3

4

5

6

7

8

9 Reflection

Uncomfortable, But Worth it:

Celebrate the Summits:

Lessons Learned / *Next Time:*

Today I am grateful for . . . Date: ....

1 ....

2 ....

3 ....

Today I am feeling . . .

....

Declare My Current Climb: ....

My 3 Summit Focus

3 MIT: (Most Important Task)

1 ....

2 ....

3 ....

Get On Belay

Who do *I* need *On Belay* today? ....

Who needs *Me On Belay* today? ....

Only as high as I reach can I grow, only as far as I seek can I go, only as deep as I look can I see, only as much as I dream can I be.

Karen Ravn

Tonight I am grateful for . . .

1 ....

2 ....

3 ....

Tonight I am gaining clarity on . . .

....

6 Clarity

7

8

9

10

11

12 Momentum

1

2

3

4

5

6

7

8

9 Reflection

Uncomfortable, But Worth it:

Celebrate the Summits:

Lessons Learned / *Next Time:*

REFLECTION > CLARITY > MOMENTUM

Consistently, ask yourself these Essential Questions and write your responses in the space provided. *When you go Deeper, You Climb Higher.*

What am I Grateful for?

What do I want More of?

Where is Resistance showing up in my life?

What might I be holding onto that I need to let go of?

What do I need to Restart?

What uncomfortable opportunity is presenting today?

Who am I Grateful for?

MY 7 SUMMIT AFFIRMATIONS

Have a long NO list, and a short YES list.

Manley Feinberg II

Today I am grateful for . . . Date: ....

1 ....

2 ....

3 ....

Today I am feeling . . .

....

Declare My Current Climb: ....

My 3 Summit Focus

3 MIT: (Most Important Task)

1 ....

2 ....

3 ....

Get On Belay

Who do *I* need *On Belay* today? ....

Who needs *Me On Belay* today? ....

Our greatest glory is not in never falling,
but in rising every time we fall.
Confucius

Tonight I am grateful for . . .

1 ....

2 ....

3 ....

Tonight I am gaining clarity on . . .

....

6 Clarity

7

8

9

10

11

12 Momentum

1

2

3

4

5

6

7

8

9 Reflection

Uncomfortable, But Worth it:

Celebrate the Summits:

Lessons Learned / *Next Time:*

Today I am grateful for . . . Date:

1

2

3

Today I am feeling . . .

Declare My Current Climb:

My 3 Summit Focus

3 MIT: (Most Important Task)

1

2

3

Get On Belay

Who do *I* need *On Belay* today?

Who needs *Me On Belay* today?

Our lives are defined by opportunities,
even the ones we miss.

F. Scott Fitzgerald

Tonight I am grateful for . . .

1

2

3

Tonight I am gaining clarity on . . .

6 Clarity

7

8

9

10

11

12 Momentum

1

2

3

4

5

6

7

8

9 Reflection

Uncomfortable, But Worth it:

Celebrate the Summits:

Lessons Learned / *Next Time:*

Today I am grateful for . . . **Date:**..

1 ....

2 ....

3 ....

Today I am feeling . . .

....

Declare My Current Climb:..

My 3 Summit Focus

3 MIT: (Most Important Task)

1 ....

2 ....

3 ....

Get On Belay

Who do *I* need *On Belay* today? ....

Who needs *Me On Belay* today?..

People often say that motivation doesn't last. Well, neither does bathing, that's why we recommend it daily.

Zig Ziglar

Tonight I am grateful for . . .

1 ....

2 ....

3 ....

Tonight I am gaining clarity on . . .

....

6 .... **Clarity**

7

8

9

10

11

12 .... **Momentum**

1

2

3

4

5

6

7

8

9 .... **Reflection**

Uncomfortable, But Worth it:

Celebrate the Summits:

Lessons Learned / *Next Time:*

Today I am grateful for . . . Date:

1

2

3

Today I am feeling . . .

Declare My Current Climb:

My 3 Summit Focus

3 MIT: (Most Important Task)

1

2

3

Get On Belay

Who do *I* need *On Belay* today?

Who needs *Me On Belay* today?

People that are hungry are willing to do the things today others won't do, in order to have the things tomorrow others won't have.

Les Brown

Tonight I am grateful for . . .

1

2

3

Tonight I am gaining clarity on . . .

6 Clarity
7
8
9
10
11
12 Momentum
1
2
3
4
5
6
7
8
9 Reflection

Uncomfortable, But Worth it:

Celebrate the Summits:

Lessons Learned / *Next Time:*

Today I am grateful for . . . **Date:** ....

1 ....

2 ....

3 ....

Today I am feeling . . .

....

Declare My Current Climb: ....

My 3 Summit Focus

3 MIT: (Most Important Task)

1 ....

2 ....

3 ....

Get On Belay

Who do *I* need *On Belay* today? ....

Who needs *Me On Belay* today? ....

Progress always involves risk. You can't steal 2nd base and keep your foot on 1st.

Fred Wilcox

Tonight I am grateful for . . .

1 ....

2 ....

3 ....

Tonight I am gaining clarity on . . .

....

6 Clarity

7

8

9

10

11

12 Momentum

1

2

3

4

5

6

7

8

9 Reflection

Uncomfortable, But Worth it:

Celebrate the Summits:

Lessons Learned / *Next Time:*

Today I am grateful for . . . Date: ....

1 ....

2 ....

3 ....

Today I am feeling . . .

....

Declare My Current Climb: ....

My 3 Summit Focus

3 MIT: (Most Important Task)

1 ....

2 ....

3 ....

Get On Belay

Who do *I* need *On Belay* today? ....

Who needs *Me On Belay* today? ....

Reach down in your gut and grab
the rest of your destiny.

Don Hutson

Tonight I am grateful for . . .

1 ....

2 ....

3 ....

Tonight I am gaining clarity on . . .

....

6 Clarity

7

8

9

10

11

12 Momentum

1

2

3

4

5

6

7

8

9 Reflection

Uncomfortable, But Worth it:

Celebrate the Summits:

Lessons Learned / *Next Time:*

Today I am grateful for . . . **Date:** ....

1 ....

2 ....

3 ....

Today I am feeling . . .

....

Declare My Current Climb: ....

My 3 Summit Focus

. . . .

. . . .

. . . .

. . . .

3 MIT: (Most Important Task)

1 ....

2 ....

3 ....

Get On Belay

Who do *I* need *On Belay* today? ....

Who needs *Me On Belay* today? ....

Remembering that you are going to die is the best way I know to avoid the trap of thinking you have something to lose.

Steve Jobs

Tonight I am grateful for . . .

1 ....

2 ....

3 ....

Tonight I am gaining clarity on . . .

....

6 Clarity

7

8

9

10

11

12 Momentum

1

2

3

4

5

6

7

8

9 Reflection

Uncomfortable, But Worth it:

Celebrate the Summits:

Lessons Learned / *Next Time:*

REFLECTION > CLARITY > MOMENTUM

Consistently, ask yourself these Essential Questions and write your responses in the space provided. *When you go Deeper, You Climb Higher.*

What am I Grateful for?

What do I want More of?

Where is Resistance showing up in my life?

What might I be holding onto that I need to let go of?

What do I need to Restart?

What uncomfortable opportunity is presenting today?

Who am I Grateful for?

MY 7 SUMMIT AFFIRMATIONS

How bad do you want it? Small choices, small decisions, small actions build massive momentum.

Manley Feinberg II

Today I am grateful for . . . Date: ....

1 ....

2 ....

3 ....

Today I am feeling . . .

....

Declare My Current Climb: ....

My 3 Summit Focus

3 MIT: (Most Important Task)

1 ....

2 ....

3 ....

Get On Belay

Who do *I* need *On Belay* today? ....

Who needs *Me On Belay* today? ....

Results are obtained by exploiting opportunities, not by solving problems.

Peter F. Drucker

Tonight I am grateful for . . .

1 ....

2 ....

3 ....

Tonight I am gaining clarity on . . .

....

6 .... **Clarity**

7

8

9

10

11

12 .... **Momentum**

1

2

3

4

5

6

7

8

9 .... **Reflection**

Uncomfortable, But Worth it:

Celebrate the Summits:

Lessons Learned / *Next Time:*

Today I am grateful for . . . **Date:**......................................

1 ....

2 ....

3 ....

Today I am feeling . . .

....

Declare My Current Climb:..

My 3 Summit Focus

. . . .

. . . .

. . . .

. . . .

3 MIT: (Most Important Task)

1 ....

2 ....

3 ....

Get On Belay

Who do *I* need *On Belay* today? ....

Who needs *Me On Belay* today?..

Success means having the courage, the determination, and the will to become the person you believe you were meant to be.

George Sheehan

Tonight I am grateful for . . .

1 ....

2 ....

3 ....

Tonight I am gaining clarity on . . .

....

6 .... **Clarity**

7

8

9

10

11

12 .... **Momentum**

1

2

3

4

5

6

7

8

9 .... **Reflection**

Uncomfortable, But Worth it:

Celebrate the Summits:

Lessons Learned / *Next Time:*

Today I am grateful for . . . Date:..

1 ....

2 ....

3 ....

Today I am feeling . . .

....

Declare My Current Climb:..

My 3 Summit Focus

3 MIT: (Most Important Task)

1 ....

2 ....

3 ....

Get On Belay

Who do *I* need *On Belay* today? ....

Who needs *Me On Belay* today?..

Success will come as a result of your commitment to excellence, intelligent planning, and focused effort.

Cathy Sexton

Tonight I am grateful for . . .

1 ....

2 ....

3 ....

Tonight I am gaining clarity on . . .

....

6 Clarity

7

8

9

10

11

12 Momentum

1

2

3

4

5

6

7

8

9 Reflection

Uncomfortable, But Worth it:

Celebrate the Summits:

Lessons Learned / *Next Time:*

Today I am grateful for . . . **Date:** ....

1 ....

2 ....

3 ....

Today I am feeling . . .

....

Declare My Current Climb: ....

My 3 Summit Focus

3 MIT: (Most Important Task)

1 ....

2 ....

3 ....

Get On Belay

Who do *I* need *On Belay* today? ....

Who needs *Me On Belay* today? ....

Take action, stay committed to your learning and mastery, and light the world with who you are.

Brendon Burchard

Tonight I am grateful for . . .

1 ....

2 ....

3 ....

Tonight I am gaining clarity on . . .

....

6 Clarity

7

8

9

10

11

12 Momentum

1

2

3

4

5

6

7

8

9 Reflection

Uncomfortable, But Worth it:

Celebrate the Summits:

Lessons Learned / *Next Time:*

Today I am grateful for . . . **Date:** ....

1 ....

2 ....

3 ....

Today I am feeling . . .

....

Declare My Current Climb: ....

My 3 Summit Focus

3 MIT: (Most Important Task)

1 ....

2 ....

3 ....

Get On Belay

Who do *I* need *On Belay* today? ....

Who needs *Me On Belay* today? ....

Take the first step in faith. You don't have to see the whole staircase. Just take the first step.

Martin Luther King, Jr.

Tonight I am grateful for . . .

1 ....

2 ....

3 ....

Tonight I am gaining clarity on . . .

....

6 Clarity

7

8

9

10

11

12 Momentum

1

2

3

4

5

6

7

8

9 Reflection

Uncomfortable, But Worth it:

Celebrate the Summits:

Lessons Learned / *Next Time:*

Today I am grateful for . . . Date:

1 ....

2 ....

3 ....

Today I am feeling . . .

....

Declare My Current Climb: ....

My 3 Summit Focus

3 MIT: (Most Important Task)

1 ....

2 ....

3 ....

Get On Belay

Who do *I* need *On Belay* today? ....

Who needs *Me On Belay* today? ....

Tell me, what is it you plan to do with your one wild and precious life?

Mary Oliver

Tonight I am grateful for . . .

1 ....

2 ....

3 ....

Tonight I am gaining clarity on . . .

....

6 Clarity

7

8

9

10

11

12 Momentum

1

2

3

4

5

6

7

8

9 Reflection

Uncomfortable, But Worth it:

Celebrate the Summits:

Lessons Learned / *Next Time:*

Today I am grateful for . . . **Date:**..

1 ....

2 ....

3 ....

Today I am feeling . . .

....

Declare My Current Climb:..

My 3 Summit Focus

3 MIT: (Most Important Task)

1 ....

2 ....

3 ....

Get On Belay

Who do *I* need *On Belay* today? ....

Who needs *Me On Belay* today?..

The deepest principle in human nature is the craving to be appreciated.

William James

Tonight I am grateful for . . .

1 ....

2 ....

3 ....

Tonight I am gaining clarity on . . .

....

6 .... Clarity

7

8

9

10

11

12 .... Momentum

1

2

3

4

5

6

7

8

9 .... Reflection

Uncomfortable, But Worth it:

Celebrate the Summits:

Lessons Learned / *Next Time:*

REFLECTION > CLARITY > MOMENTUM

Consistently, ask yourself these Essential Questions and write your responses in the space provided. *When you go Deeper, You Climb Higher.*

What am I Grateful for?

What do I want More of?

Where is Resistance showing up in my life?

What might I be holding onto that I need to let go of?

What do I need to Restart?

What uncomfortable opportunity is presenting today?

Who am I Grateful for?

MY 7 SUMMIT AFFIRMATIONS

I'm too excited by the summit to put off the moves that are taking me there.

Manley Feinberg II

Today I am grateful for . . . Date: ....

1 ....

2 ....

3 ....

Today I am feeling . . .

....

Declare My Current Climb: ....

My 3 Summit Focus

3 MIT: (Most Important Task)

1 ....

2 ....

3 ....

Get On Belay

Who do *I* need *On Belay* today? ....

Who needs *Me On Belay* today? ....

The future you see is the future you get.

Robert G. Allen

Tonight I am grateful for . . .

1 ....

2 ....

3 ....

Tonight I am gaining clarity on . . .

....

6 Clarity

7

8

9

10

11

12 Momentum

1

2

3

4

5

6

7

8

9 Reflection

Uncomfortable, But Worth it:

Celebrate the Summits:

Lessons Learned / *Next Time:*

Today I am grateful for . . . Date: ....

1 ....

2 ....

3 ....

Today I am feeling . . .

....

Declare My Current Climb: ....

My 3 Summit Focus

3 MIT: (Most Important Task)

1 ....

2 ....

3 ....

Get On Belay

Who do *I* need *On Belay* today? ....

Who needs *Me On Belay* today? ....

The greatest weapon against stress is our ability to choose one thought over another.

William James

Tonight I am grateful for . . .

1 ....

2 ....

3 ....

Tonight I am gaining clarity on . . .

....

6 .... Clarity

7

8

9

10

11

12 .... Momentum

1

2

3

4

5

6

7

8

9 .... Reflection

Uncomfortable, But Worth it:

Celebrate the Summits:

Lessons Learned / *Next Time:*

Today I am grateful for . . . **Date:** ....

1 ....

2 ....

3 ....

Today I am feeling . . .

....

Declare My Current Climb: ....

My 3 Summit Focus

3 MIT: (Most Important Task)

1 ....

2 ....

3 ....

Get On Belay

Who do *I* need *On Belay* today? ....

Who needs *Me On Belay* today? ....

The more important a call or action is to our soul's evolution, the more Resistance we will feel toward pursuing it.

Stephen Pressfield

Tonight I am grateful for . . .

1 ....

2 ....

3 ....

Tonight I am gaining clarity on . . .

....

6 Clarity

7

8

9

10

11

12 Momentum

1

2

3

4

5

6

7

8

9 Reflection

Uncomfortable, But Worth it:

Celebrate the Summits:

Lessons Learned / *Next Time:*

Today I am grateful for . . . Date: ....

1 ....

2 ....

3 ....

Today I am feeling . . .

....

Declare My Current Climb: ....

My 3 Summit Focus

3 MIT: (Most Important Task)

1 ....

2 ....

3 ....

Get On Belay

Who do *I* need *On Belay* today? ....

Who needs *Me On Belay* today? ....

The most powerful weapon on earth is the human soul on fire.

Ferdinand Foch

Tonight I am grateful for . . .

1 ....

2 ....

3 ....

Tonight I am gaining clarity on . . .

....

6 Clarity

7

8

9

10

11

12 Momentum

1

2

3

4

5

6

7

8

9 Reflection

Uncomfortable, But Worth it:

Celebrate the Summits:

Lessons Learned / *Next Time:*

Today I am grateful for . . . Date: ....

1 ....

2 ....

3 ....

Today I am feeling . . .

....

Declare My Current Climb: ....

My 3 Summit Focus

3 MIT: (Most Important Task)

1 ....

2 ....

3 ....

Get On Belay

Who do *I* need *On Belay* today? ....

Who needs *Me On Belay* today? ....

The only difference in a rut and a grave are the dimensions.

Keith Harrell

Tonight I am grateful for . . .

1 ....

2 ....

3 ....

Tonight I am gaining clarity on . . .

....

6 Clarity

7

8

9

10

11

12 Momentum

1

2

3

4

5

6

7

8

9 Reflection

Uncomfortable, But Worth it:

Celebrate the Summits:

Lessons Learned / *Next Time:*

Today I am grateful for . . . Date: ....

1 ....

2 ....

3 ....

Today I am feeling . . .

....

Declare My Current Climb: ....

My 3 Summit Focus

3 MIT: (Most Important Task)

1 ....

2 ....

3 ....

Get On Belay

Who do *I* need *On Belay* today? ....

Who needs *Me On Belay* today? ....

The outer conditions of a person's life will always be found to reflect their inner beliefs.

James Allen

Tonight I am grateful for . . .

1 ....

2 ....

3 ....

Tonight I am gaining clarity on . . .

....

6 Clarity

7

8

9

10

11

12 Momentum

1

2

3

4

5

6

7

8

9 Reflection

Uncomfortable, But Worth it:

Celebrate the Summits:

Lessons Learned / *Next Time:*

Today I am grateful for . . . Date: ....

1 ....

2 ....

3 ....

Today I am feeling . . .

....

Declare My Current Climb: ....

My 3 Summit Focus

3 MIT: (Most Important Task)

1 ....

2 ....

3 ....

Get On Belay

Who do *I* need *On Belay* today? ....

Who needs *Me On Belay* today? ....

The secret to happiness is freedom. And the secret to freedom is courage.

Thucydides

Tonight I am grateful for . . .

1 ....

2 ....

3 ....

Tonight I am gaining clarity on . . .

....

6 Clarity

7

8

9

10

11

12 Momentum

1

2

3

4

5

6

7

8

9 Reflection

Uncomfortable, But Worth it:

Celebrate the Summits:

Lessons Learned / *Next Time:*

REFLECTION > CLARITY > MOMENTUM

Consistently, ask yourself these Essential Questions and write your responses in the space provided. *When you go Deeper, You Climb Higher.*

What am I Grateful for?

What do I want More of?

Where is Resistance showing up in my life?

What might I be holding onto that I need to let go of?

What do I need to Restart?

What uncomfortable opportunity is presenting today?

Who am I Grateful for?

MY 7 SUMMIT AFFIRMATIONS

Now is not too late, but tomorrow might be.

Manley Feinberg II

Today I am grateful for . . . Date:...................................

1 ....

2 ....

3 ....

Today I am feeling . . .

....

Declare My Current Climb:..

My 3 Summit Focus

3 MIT: (Most Important Task)

1 ....

2 ....

3 ....

Get On Belay

Who do *I* need *On Belay* today?..

Who needs *Me On Belay* today?..

Those who turn back know only the ordeal, but they who persevere remember the adventure.

Milo L. Arnold

Tonight I am grateful for . . .

1 ....

2 ....

3 ....

Tonight I am gaining clarity on . . .

....

6 Clarity

7

8

9

10

11

12 Momentum

1

2

3

4

5

6

7

8

9 Reflection

Uncomfortable, But Worth it:

Celebrate the Summits:

Lessons Learned / *Next Time:*

Today I am grateful for . . . **Date:** ....

1 ....

2 ....

3 ....

Today I am feeling . . .

....

Declare My Current Climb: ....

My 3 Summit Focus

3 MIT: (Most Important Task)

1 ....

2 ....

3 ....

Get On Belay

Who do *I* need *On Belay* today? ....

Who needs *Me On Belay* today? ....

There are two primary choices in life: to accept conditions as they exist, or accept the responsibility for changing them.

Denis Waitley

Tonight I am grateful for . . .

1 ....

2 ....

3 ....

Tonight I am gaining clarity on . . .

....

6 Clarity

7

8

9

10

11

12 Momentum

1

2

3

4

5

6

7

8

9 Reflection

Uncomfortable, But Worth it:

Celebrate the Summits:

Lessons Learned / *Next Time:*

Today I am grateful for . . . Date:

1

2

3

Today I am feeling . . .

Declare My Current Climb:

My 3 Summit Focus

3 MIT: (Most Important Task)

1

2

3

Get On Belay

Who do *I* need *On Belay* today?

Who needs *Me On Belay* today?

There is great comfort in remembering that I don't have to be brave and courageous every minute of my life. 20 seconds here and there will do.

Jason Koteki

Tonight I am grateful for . . .

1

2

3

Tonight I am gaining clarity on . . .

6 .... Clarity

7

8

9

10

11

12 .... Momentum

1

2

3

4

5

6

7

8

9 .... Reflection

Uncomfortable, But Worth it:

Celebrate the Summits:

Lessons Learned / *Next Time:*

Today I am grateful for . . . Date: ....

1 ....

2 ....

3 ....

Today I am feeling . . .

....

Declare My Current Climb: ....

My 3 Summit Focus

3 MIT: (Most Important Task)

1 ....

2 ....

3 ....

Get On Belay

Who do *I* need *On Belay* today? ....

Who needs *Me On Belay* today? ....

There is no passion to be found playing small, in settling for a life that is less than the one you are capable of living.

Nelson Mandela

Tonight I am grateful for . . .

1 ....

2 ....

3 ....

Tonight I am gaining clarity on . . .

....

6 .... Clarity

7

8

9

10

11

12 .... Momentum

1

2

3

4

5

6

7

8

9 .... Reflection

Uncomfortable, But Worth it:

Celebrate the Summits:

Lessons Learned / *Next Time:*

Today I am grateful for . . . **Date:**..

1 ....

2 ....

3 ....

Today I am feeling . . .

....

Declare My Current Climb:..

My 3 Summit Focus

3 MIT: (Most Important Task)

1 ....

2 ....

3 ....

Get On Belay

Who do *I* need *On Belay* today? ....

Who needs *Me On Belay* today?..

There is nothing with which every man is afraid as getting to know how enormously much he is capable of doing and becoming.

Soren Kierkegaard

Tonight I am grateful for . . .

1 ....

2 ....

3 ....

Tonight I am gaining clarity on . . .

....

6 Clarity
7
8
9
10
11
12 Momentum
1
2
3
4
5
6
7
8
9 Reflection

Uncomfortable, But Worth it:

Celebrate the Summits:

Lessons Learned / *Next Time:*

Today I am grateful for . . . Date: ....

1 ....

2 ....

3 ....

Today I am feeling . . .

....

Declare My Current Climb: ....

My 3 Summit Focus

3 MIT: (Most Important Task)

1 ....

2 ....

3 ....

Get On Belay

Who do *I* need *On Belay* today? ....

Who needs *Me On Belay* today? ....

There is someone out there half as good as you working twice as hard.

Darren LaCroix

Tonight I am grateful for . . .

1 ....

2 ....

3 ....

Tonight I am gaining clarity on . . .

....

6 Clarity

7

8

9

10

11

12 Momentum

1

2

3

4

5

6

7

8

9 Reflection

Uncomfortable, But Worth it:

Celebrate the Summits:

Lessons Learned / *Next Time:*

Today I am grateful for . . . Date:.................................

1 ....

2 ....

3 ....

Today I am feeling . . .

....

Declare My Current Climb:..

My 3 Summit Focus

3 MIT: (Most Important Task)

1 ....

2 ....

3 ....

Get On Belay

Who do *I* need *On Belay* today? ....

Who needs *Me On Belay* today?..

There are only two times in life,
NOW & TOO LATE!

Terry Hawkins

Tonight I am grateful for . . .

1 ....

2 ....

3 ....

Tonight I am gaining clarity on . . .

....

6 .... **Clarity**

7

8

9

10

11

12 .... **Momentum**

1

2

3

4

5

6

7

8

9 .... **Reflection**

Uncomfortable, But Worth it:

Celebrate the Summits:

Lessons Learned / *Next Time:*

REFLECTION > CLARITY > MOMENTUM

Consistently, ask yourself these Essential Questions and write your responses in the space provided. *When you go Deeper, You Climb Higher.*

What am I Grateful for?

What do I want More of?

Where is Resistance showing up in my life?

What might I be holding onto that I need to let go of?

What do I need to Restart?

What uncomfortable opportunity is presenting today?

Who am I Grateful for?

MY 7 SUMMIT AFFIRMATIONS

Visibility Drives Velocity.

Manley Feinberg II

Today I am grateful for . . . Date: ....

1 ....

2 ....

3 ....

Today I am feeling . . .

....

Declare My Current Climb: ....

My 3 Summit Focus

3 MIT: (Most Important Task)

1 ....

2 ....

3 ....

Get On Belay

Who do *I* need *On Belay* today? ....

Who needs *Me On Belay* today? ....

Time is more valuable than money. You can get more money, but you cannot get more time.

Jim Rohn

Tonight I am grateful for . . .

1 ....

2 ....

3 ....

Tonight I am gaining clarity on . . .

....

6 Clarity

7

8

9

10

11

12 Momentum

1

2

3

4

5

6

7

8

9 Reflection

Uncomfortable, But Worth it:

Celebrate the Summits:

Lessons Learned / *Next Time:*

Today I am grateful for . . .   Date: ....

1 ....

2 ....

3 ....

Today I am feeling . . .

....

Declare My Current Climb: ....

My 3 Summit Focus

3 MIT: (Most Important Task)

1 ....

2 ....

3 ....

Get On Belay

Who do *I* need *On Belay* today? ....

Who needs *Me On Belay* today? ....

Vision without action is daydream.
Action without vision is nightmare.

Japanese Proverb

Tonight I am grateful for . . .

1 ....

2 ....

3 ....

Tonight I am gaining clarity on . . .

....

6 Clarity

7

8

9

10

11

12 Momentum

1

2

3

4

5

6

7

8

9 Reflection

Uncomfortable, But Worth it:

Celebrate the Summits:

Lessons Learned / *Next Time:*

Today I am grateful for . . . Date:..

1 ....

2 ....

3 ....

Today I am feeling . . .

....

Declare My Current Climb:..

My 3 Summit Focus

3 MIT: (Most Important Task)

1 ....

2 ....

3 ....

Get On Belay

Who do *I* need *On Belay* today? ....

Who needs *Me On Belay* today?..

Watch your thoughts, for they become words. Watch your words, for they become actions. Watch your actions, for they become habits. Watch your habits, for they become character. Watch your character, for it becomes your destiny.

Frank Outlaw

Tonight I am grateful for . . .

1 ....

2 ....

3 ....

Tonight I am gaining clarity on . . .

....

6 Clarity

7

8

9

10

11

12 Momentum

1

2

3

4

5

6

7

8

9 Reflection

Uncomfortable, But Worth it:

Celebrate the Summits:

Lessons Learned / *Next Time:*

Today I am grateful for . . . Date: ....

1 ....

2 ....

3 ....

Today I am feeling . . .

....

Declare My Current Climb: ....

My 3 Summit Focus

3 MIT: (Most Important Task)

1 ....

2 ....

3 ....

Get On Belay

Who do *I* need *On Belay* today? ....

Who needs *Me On Belay* today? ....

We are what we repeatedly do.
Excellence, then, is not an act, but a habit!

Aristotle

Tonight I am grateful for . . .

1 ....

2 ....

3 ....

Tonight I am gaining clarity on . . .

....

6 Clarity

7

8

9

10

11

12 Momentum

1

2

3

4

5

6

7

8

9 Reflection

Uncomfortable, But Worth it:

Celebrate the Summits:

Lessons Learned / *Next Time:*

Today I am grateful for . . . Date: ....

1 ....

2 ....

3 ....

Today I am feeling . . .

....

Declare My Current Climb: ....

My 3 Summit Focus

3 MIT: (Most Important Task)

1 ....

2 ....

3 ....

Get On Belay

Who do *I* need *On Belay* today? ....

Who needs *Me On Belay* today? ....

We aren't half afraid of dying as we are that no one will remember that we were ever here.

LaShunda Rundles

Tonight I am grateful for . . .

1 ....

2 ....

3 ....

Tonight I am gaining clarity on . . .

....

6 Clarity

7

8

9

10

11

12 Momentum

1

2

3

4

5

6

7

8

9 Reflection

Uncomfortable, But Worth it:

Celebrate the Summits:

Lessons Learned / *Next Time:*

Today I am grateful for . . . **Date:** ....

1 ....

2 ....

3 ....

Today I am feeling . . .

....

Declare My Current Climb: ....

My 3 Summit Focus

3 MIT: (Most Important Task)

1 ....

2 ....

3 ....

Get On Belay

Who do *I* need *On Belay* today? ....

Who needs *Me On Belay* today? ....

We generally change ourselves for one of two reasons: inspiration or desperation.

Jim Rohn

Tonight I am grateful for . . .

1 ....

2 ....

3 ....

Tonight I am gaining clarity on . . .

....

6 Clarity

7

8

9

10

11

12 Momentum

1

2

3

4

5

6

7

8

9 Reflection

Uncomfortable, But Worth it:

Celebrate the Summits:

Lessons Learned / *Next Time:*

Today I am grateful for . . . Date: ....

1 ....

2 ....

3 ....

Today I am feeling . . .

....

Declare My Current Climb: ....

My 3 Summit Focus

3 MIT: (Most Important Task)

1 ....

2 ....

3 ....

Get On Belay

Who do *I* need *On Belay* today? ....

Who needs *Me On Belay* today? ....

We make a living by what we get but we make a life by what we give.

Winston Churchill

Tonight I am grateful for . . .

1 ....

2 ....

3 ....

Tonight I am gaining clarity on . . .

....

6 Clarity

7

8

9

10

11

12 Momentum

1

2

3

4

5

6

7

8

9 Reflection

Uncomfortable, But Worth it:

Celebrate the Summits:

Lessons Learned / *Next Time:*

REFLECTION > CLARITY > MOMENTUM

Consistently, ask yourself these Essential Questions and write your responses in the space provided. *When you go Deeper, You Climb Higher.*

What am I Grateful for?

What do I want More of?

Where is Resistance showing up in my life?

What might I be holding onto that I need to let go of?

What do I need to Restart?

What uncomfortable opportunity is presenting today?

Who am I Grateful for?

MY 7 SUMMIT AFFIRMATIONS

You always hit the wall before
you gain the summit.

Manley Feinberg II

Today I am grateful for . . . Date: ....

1 ....

2 ....

3 ....

Today I am feeling . . .

....

Declare My Current Climb: ....

My 3 Summit Focus

3 MIT: (Most Important Task)

1 ....

2 ....

3 ....

Get On Belay

Who do *I* need *On Belay* today? ....

Who needs *Me On Belay* today? ....

What would you dare to dream if you knew you wouldn't fail?

Brian Tracy

Tonight I am grateful for . . .

1 ....

2 ....

3 ....

Tonight I am gaining clarity on . . .

....

6 .... Clarity

7

8

9

10

11

12 .... Momentum

1

2

3

4

5

6

7

8

9 .... Reflection

Uncomfortable, But Worth it:

Celebrate the Summits:

Lessons Learned / *Next Time:*

Today I am grateful for . . . **Date:** ....

1 ....

2 ....

3 ....

Today I am feeling . . .

....

Declare My Current Climb: ....

My 3 Summit Focus

3 MIT: (Most Important Task)

1 ....

2 ....

3 ....

Get On Belay

Who do *I* need *On Belay* today? ....

Who needs *Me On Belay* today? ....

What you do everyday is more important than what you do once in a while.

Mark LeBlanc

Tonight I am grateful for . . .

1 ....

2 ....

3 ....

Tonight I am gaining clarity on . . .

....

6 Clarity

7

8

9

10

11

12 Momentum

1

2

3

4

5

6

7

8

9 Reflection

Uncomfortable, But Worth it:

Celebrate the Summits:

Lessons Learned / *Next Time:*

Today I am grateful for . . . Date: ....

1 ....

2 ....

3 ....

Today I am feeling . . .

....

Declare My Current Climb: ....

My 3 Summit Focus

3 MIT: (Most Important Task)

1 ....

2 ....

3 ....

Get On Belay

Who do *I* need *On Belay* today? ....

Who needs *Me On Belay* today? ....

What you resist persist.

Carl Jung

Tonight I am grateful for . . .

1 ....

2 ....

3 ....

Tonight I am gaining clarity on . . .

....

6 Clarity

7

8

9

10

11

12 Momentum

1

2

3

4

5

6

7

8

9 Reflection

Uncomfortable, But Worth it:

Celebrate the Summits:

Lessons Learned / *Next Time:*

Today I am grateful for . . . Date: ....

1 ....

2 ....

3 ....

Today I am feeling . . .

....

Declare My Current Climb: ....

My 3 Summit Focus

3 MIT: (Most Important Task)

1 ....

2 ....

3 ....

Get On Belay

Who do *I* need *On Belay* today? ....

Who needs *Me On Belay* today? ....

Whatever you're thinking, think bigger.

Tony Hsieh

Tonight I am grateful for . . .

1 ....

2 ....

3 ....

Tonight I am gaining clarity on . . .

....

6 Clarity

7

8

9

10

11

12 Momentum

1

2

3

4

5

6

7

8

9 Reflection

Uncomfortable, But Worth it:

Celebrate the Summits:

Lessons Learned / *Next Time:*

Today I am grateful for . . . Date: ....

1 ....

2 ....

3 ....

Today I am feeling . . .

....

Declare My Current Climb: ....

My 3 Summit Focus

3 MIT: (Most Important Task)

1 ....

2 ....

3 ....

Get On Belay

Who do *I* need *On Belay* today? ....

Who needs *Me On Belay* today? ....

When I began my journey to learn how to make people laugh I did not have brains, talent, connections, or money. All I had was persistence. Turns out that's all you need.

Darren LaCroix

Tonight I am grateful for . . .

1 ....

2 ....

3 ....

Tonight I am gaining clarity on . . .

....

6 .... Clarity

7

8

9

10

11

12 .... Momentum

1

2

3

4

5

6

7

8

9 .... Reflection

Uncomfortable, But Worth it:

Celebrate the Summits:

Lessons Learned / *Next Time:*

Today I am grateful for . . . **Date:** ....

1 ....
2 ....
3 ....

Today I am feeling . . .

....

Declare My Current Climb: ....

My 3 Summit Focus

3 MIT: (Most Important Task)

1 ....
2 ....
3 ....

Get On Belay

Who do *I* need *On Belay* today? ....

Who needs *Me On Belay* today? ....

When the Pain of the Same is Greater than the Pain of the Change, the Change will come!

Fred Pryor

Tonight I am grateful for . . .

1 ....
2 ....
3 ....

Tonight I am gaining clarity on . . .

....

6 Clarity

7

8

9

10

11

12 Momentum

1

2

3

4

5

6

7

8

9 Reflection

Uncomfortable, But Worth it:

Celebrate the Summits:

Lessons Learned / *Next Time:*

Today I am grateful for . . . **Date:**.....................................

1 ....

2 ....

3 ....

Today I am feeling . . .

....

Declare My Current Climb:...

My 3 Summit Focus

3 MIT: (Most Important Task)

1 ....

2 ....

3 ....

Get On Belay

Who do *I* need *On Belay* today? ....

Who needs *Me On Belay* today?...

Yesterday's consistency predicts tomorrow's profitability.

Scott Ginsberg

Tonight I am grateful for . . .

1 ....

2 ....

3 ....

Tonight I am gaining clarity on . . .

....

6 Clarity

7

8

9

10

11

12 Momentum

1

2

3

4

5

6

7

8

9 Reflection

Uncomfortable, But Worth it:

Celebrate the Summits:

Lessons Learned / *Next Time:*

REFLECTION > CLARITY > MOMENTUM

Consistently, ask yourself these Essential Questions and write your responses in the space provided. *When you go Deeper, You Climb Higher.*

What am I Grateful for?

What do I want More of?

Where is Resistance showing up in my life?

What might I be holding onto that I need to let go of?

What do I need to Restart?

What uncomfortable opportunity is presenting today?

Who am I Grateful for?

MY 7 SUMMIT AFFIRMATIONS

You can't settle for less when you know there is something more.

Manley Feinberg II

Today I am grateful for . . .   Date: ....

1 ....

2 ....

3 ....

Today I am feeling . . .

....

Declare My Current Climb: ....

My 3 Summit Focus

3 MIT: (Most Important Task)

1 ....

2 ....

3 ....

Get On Belay

Who do *I* need *On Belay* today? ....

Who needs *Me On Belay* today? ....

When we conquer our fears, we discover a boundless, bottomless, inexhaustible well of passion.

Stephen Pressfield

Tonight I am grateful for . . .

1 ....

2 ....

3 ....

Tonight I am gaining clarity on . . .

....

6 .... Clarity

7

8

9

10

11

12 .... Momentum

1

2

3

4

5

6

7

8

9 .... Reflection

Uncomfortable, But Worth it:

Celebrate the Summits:

Lessons Learned / *Next Time:*

Today I am grateful for . . . **Date:** ....

1 ....

2 ....

3 ....

Today I am feeling . . .

....

Declare My Current Climb: ....

My 3 Summit Focus

3 MIT: (Most Important Task)

1 ....

2 ....

3 ....

Get On Belay

Who do *I* need *On Belay* today? ....

Who needs *Me On Belay* today? ....

When you are not practicing, someone else is.
When you meet him, he will win.

Martial Arts Proverb

Tonight I am grateful for . . .

1 ....

2 ....

3 ....

Tonight I am gaining clarity on . . .

....

6 Clarity

7

8

9

10

11

12 Momentum

1

2

3

4

5

6

7

8

9 Reflection

Uncomfortable, But Worth it:

Celebrate the Summits:

Lessons Learned / *Next Time:*

Today I am grateful for . . . Date: ....

1 ....

2 ....

3 ....

Today I am feeling . . .

....

Declare My Current Climb: ....

My 3 Summit Focus

3 MIT: (Most Important Task)

1 ....

2 ....

3 ....

Get On Belay

Who do *I* need *On Belay* today? ....

Who needs *Me On Belay* today? ....

With a made up mind, there's no more maybe.

Craig Valentine

Tonight I am grateful for . . .

1 ....

2 ....

3 ....

Tonight I am gaining clarity on . . .

....

6 .... **Clarity**

7

8

9

10

11

12 .... **Momentum**

1

2

3

4

5

6

7

8

9 .... **Reflection**

Uncomfortable, But Worth it:

Celebrate the Summits:

Lessons Learned / *Next Time:*

Today I am grateful for . . . Date: ....

1 ....

2 ....

3 ....

Today I am feeling . . .

....

Declare My Current Climb: ....

My 3 Summit Focus

3 MIT: (Most Important Task)

1 ....

2 ....

3 ....

Get On Belay

Who do *I* need *On Belay* today? ....

Who needs *Me On Belay* today? ....

You become what you think about most of the time.

Earl Nightingale

Tonight I am grateful for . . .

1 ....

2 ....

3 ....

Tonight I am gaining clarity on . . .

....

6 ....Clarity

7

8

9

10

11

12 ....Momentum

1

2

3

4

5

6

7

8

9 ....Reflection

Uncomfortable, But Worth it:

Celebrate the Summits:

Lessons Learned / *Next Time:*

Today I am grateful for . . . **Date:**

1 ....

2 ....

3 ....

Today I am feeling . . .

....

Declare My Current Climb:..........

My 3 Summit Focus

3 MIT: (Most Important Task)

1 ....

2 ....

3 ....

Get On Belay

Who do *I* need *On Belay* today? ....

Who needs *Me On Belay* today?..........

You miss 100% of the shots you never take.

Wayne Gretsky

Tonight I am grateful for . . .

1 ....

2 ....

3 ....

Tonight I am gaining clarity on . . .

....

6 Clarity

7

8

9

10

11

12 Momentum

1

2

3

4

5

6

7

8

9 Reflection

Uncomfortable, But Worth it:

Celebrate the Summits:

Lessons Learned / *Next Time:*

Today I am grateful for . . . Date:

1

2

3

Today I am feeling . . .

Declare My Current Climb:

My 3 Summit Focus

3 MIT: (Most Important Task)

1

2

3

Get On Belay

Who do *I* need *On Belay* today?

Who needs *Me On Belay* today?

Your attitude, not your aptitude,
will determine your altitude.

Zig Ziglar

Tonight I am grateful for . . .

1

2

3

Tonight I am gaining clarity on . . .

6 Clarity

7

8

9

10

11

12 Momentum

1

2

3

4

5

6

7

8

9 Reflection

Uncomfortable, But Worth it:

Celebrate the Summits:

Lessons Learned / *Next Time:*

Today I am grateful for . . . **Date:**..............................

1 ....

2 ....

3 ....

Today I am feeling . . .

....

Declare My Current Climb:..

My 3 Summit Focus

3 MIT: (Most Important Task)

1 ....

2 ....

3 ....

Get On Belay

Who do *I* need *On Belay* today? ....

Who needs *Me On Belay* today?..

You're off to Great Places! Today is your day!
Your mountain is waiting, so…get on your way!
Dr. Seuss

Tonight I am grateful for . . .

1 ....

2 ....

3 ....

Tonight I am gaining clarity on . . .

....

6 Clarity

7

8

9

10

11

12 Momentum

1

2

3

4

5

6

7

8

9 Reflection

Uncomfortable, But Worth it:

Celebrate the Summits:

Lessons Learned / *Next Time:*

REFLECTION > CLARITY > MOMENTUM

Consistently, ask yourself these Essential Questions and write your responses in the space provided. *When you go Deeper, You Climb Higher.*

What am I Grateful for?

What do I want More of?

Where is Resistance showing up in my life?

What might I be holding onto that I need to let go of?

What do I need to Restart?

What uncomfortable opportunity is presenting today?

Who am I Grateful for?

MY 7 SUMMIT AFFIRMATIONS

Your Win is waiting on Your When. And your When is Waiting on YOU!

Manley Feinberg II

CELEBRATE THE SUMMITS!

Date: Summit:

CELEBRATE THE SUMMITS!

Date: Summit:

CELEBRATE THE SUMMITS!

Date: Summit:

CELEBRATE THE SUMMITS!

Date: Summit:

CELEBRATE THE SUMMITS!

Date: Summit:

CELEBRATE THE SUMMITS!

Date: Summit:

CELEBRATE THE SUMMITS!

Date: Summit:

CELEBRATE THE SUMMITS!

Date: Summit:

CELEBRATE THE SUMMITS!

Date: Summit:

CELEBRATE THE SUMMITS!

Date: Summit:

CELEBRATE THE SUMMITS!

Date: Summit:

CELEBRATE THE SUMMITS!

Date: **Summit:**

CELEBRATE THE SUMMITS!

Date: Summit:

CELEBRATE THE SUMMITS!

Date: Summit:

BOOK MANLEY TO SPEAK

Are you looking for an engaging and meaningful way to kick off or close your annual meeting or event?

Manley's unforgettable keynote programs will equip you with content you can use immediately, and also inspire you to actually step up with more focus, more commitment, and more momentum when you walk out the door. Regardless of your title, Manley's Vertical Lessons will help you build stronger relationships, develop more engaged teams, and lead with courage to realize greater results in your work and life.

"Best keynote speaker I've ever heard!"

Tom Moen, Solutions Specialist, Microsoft

"Manley inspired and equipped our sales and marketing teams to achieve breakthrough Q3 / Q4 results. His message and content were customized and relevant so that it inspired my team to put it into action. His content is based on real results he's achieved in business—not theory. We enjoyed him so much, that we immediately re-hired him to work with more of our teams across the whole company."

Jim Norton, EVP Sales & Marketing, Bomgar

"Manley inspired and connected to our June 2015 audience of Energizer global leaders. The preparation by Manley to learn about our company in order to customize his message made a huge difference. I would highly recommend Manley as an inspirational speaker for leadership events.

Sue Drath, VP Global Rewards, Energizer

Get On Belay with Manley today to start a conversation on how a custom program can help you Reach Your Next Summit:

Let's stay connected:

VerticalLessons.com
Human Voice: 314-724-3443
Manley@VerticalLessons.com

VerticalLessons.com/LinkedIn
VerticalLessons.com/Facebook
VerticalLessons.com/YouTube

Whatever you can do or dream you can, begin it. Boldness has genius, power and magic in it. Begin it now!

Johan Wolfgang von Goethe

Get your FREE Training and Support to Accelerate Your Results with Your Momentum Journal: VerticalMomentum.com

To reorder go to VerticalMomentum.com

On Belay,